Passion before Prudence

Commitment is the Mother of Meaning

RICHARD M. GRAY

WESTBOW·
PRESS
A DIVISION OF THOMAS NELSON
& ZONDERVAN

WestBow Press books may be ordered through booksellers or by contacting:

WestBow Press
A Division of Thomas Nelson & Zondervan
1663 Liberty Drive
Bloomington, IN 47403
www.westbowpress.com
1 (866) 928-1240

ISBN: 978-1-4908-4358-2 (sc)
ISBN: 978-1-4908-4359-9 (e)

Library of Congress Control Number: 2014912189

Printed in the United States of America.

WestBow Press rev. date: 7/21/2014

For Catherine, my loving wife of 70 years, from her twenties to her nineties, and my life-long companion in commitment

I n the 1800's, when Danish existentialist Soren Kierkegaard was a young man, he wrote in his journal: "What I really lack is to be clear in my mind *what I am to do.* The thing is to understand myself, to see what God really wishes me to do; the thing is to find a truth which is *true for me, to find the idea for which I can live and die.*"

We all need a purpose in life. Life without purpose is empty. Looking back over the years, it seems to me that much of my life has been a quest for commitments which will give life meaning.

Discovering meaning in our lives is more than an intellectual exercise. Since we have progressed (or regressed) as a culture from the benefits of meanings which are shared with others to the necessity of finding meaning on our own, its discovery has become a singular challenge.

Based on Husserl's definition of meaning as an intention of the mind, author Rollo May found the roots of meaning in "intentionality," which he described as the capacity to have intentions and which he believed underlies both our conscious and unconscious intentions. "Intentionality," wrote May, "is the structure which gives meaning to experience."

He believed further that every intention is a "stretching toward something."

I concur. While animals have instincts, humans have intentions, and it's around those intentions that we organize our lives.

The "doctor of meaning" in our times was psychologist Viktor Frankl, founder of *logotherapy* (or meaning therapy). In his landmark work with holocaust survivors, Frankl concluded that we are "dominated not by the will to pleasure (as Sigmund Freud posited) nor by the will to power (as Alfred Adler contended) but by the will to meaning." In his study of holocaust survivors, Frankl found, as Nietsche wrote, that we can endure almost any *how* if we have a *why*.

Meaning, in short, is what we live for. And meaning is what we may be willing to die for.

Maurice Merleau-Ponty wrote that "because we are present to a world, we are condemned to meaning." Huston Smith chose that phrase for the title of his provocative book, *Condemned to Meaning*.

Can one have meaning without intentions? I don't think so. Intentions are what lead us toward one thing or another, toward one person or another. They are, as May suggested, a "stretching toward something." In

Kierkegaard's words, "persistent striving is the ethical life view of the (individual)." And every stretching or striving has within it a commitment. So if it is intentionality which propels us toward commitments, it is commitments which enable us to find meaning.

If that premise is true, i.e. if commitment is the path to meaning, it follows that the nature and quality of our commitments will determine the nature and quality of our lives. It can even be said that our commitments determine who it is we will become.

The most creative, courageous acts and the most evil, destructive deeds are carried out in pursuit of meaning. That's because human beings are compulsive meaning-makers.

On the positive side, consider the firefighter who enters a burning building to save a child. He doesn't know what the outcome will be, for himself or the child. But his commitment to do what he feels called to do is greater than it is for the safety of his own life. And in making that commitment he is also making meaning.

On the negative side, consider the suicide-bomber. Through fasting and prayer he prepares himself for his task. He may be immature and uncritical in his thinking. His values may be twisted. But in his strange and perverted quest, he makes the commitment to destroy others – and himself -- in the pursuit of meaning.

Most of our commitments are not that dramatic. But taken as a whole, they serve to define our lives.

What *kinds* of commitments do we make? Freud suggested that the keys to fulfillment are the capacities to work and to love. And while I believe Freud was wrong on many points, he was surely right about these. But in place of work and love I would use the more inclusive terms of *agency* and *communion* or *actuation* and *participation*.

The Twin Paths of Commitment

These, I believe, are the two innate strivings that govern how we function as human beings. In his book, *The Duality of Human Existence*, David Bakan called these two strivings or motivations "agency" and "communion." For now, let's call them "actuation" and "participation."

By *actuation* I mean the striving of the individual to influence, manage, or master his or her environment, whether that environment is personal, as it is in the social world, or transpersonal, as it is in the natural world. *Actuation* is a motivational thrust, a directional trend. The goal toward which it strives is what Robert White calls "effectance." Its means of attaining that goal is some form of competence.

Participation is also an innate, active, original striving. But its goal is connection, fusion, or belonging. And its means of attaining that goal are communication, engagement, association.

Since these two strivings lead in opposite directions, there is inevitably tension between the two. How do we resolve that tension? The answer is that we don't. That tension, in fact, is the source of our development as human beings. The tension is why an emphasis on one striving tends to follow the other.

What Otto Rank called the "trauma of birth," an act of agency or actuation (marked by breathing for the first time on one's own), follows communion or participation in the life of the mother, in the womb.

In the same way, nursing, an act of participation, is followed by the infant's mastery of the crib environment with hands or mouth and, ultimately, by a process of weaning to solid foods, both of which are acts of agency.

This rhythm between the strivings for actuation and participation continues throughout life. Tension between the two is desirable because excessive actuation can lead to *isolation* (Bakan cites Hitler as an example of agency unmitigated by communion) and excessive participation (consider Jonestown) can lead to *incorporation* by another or others.

Psychologist Erik Erickson does not use these terms in describing his eight stages of human development. But his analysis charts a life-long alternation between the two.

Life begins, writes Erickson, with the stage of *trust*, a stage of participation or communion, before we develop *autonomy*, a stage of actuation or agency. Autonomy is followed by the working through of relationships with parents during the stage of *initiative* to the achievement of what Erickson calls *industry*. We must then acquire *identity* before we can move to the joys and responsibilities of *intimacy*. Next comes the creative stage of *generativity*, followed by an integration through our "comradeship with distant times" to the final stage of *integrity*.

This oscillation between actuation and participation is due to the fact that human beings are innately both agents and participants, that our strivings are in both directions, one usually alternating with the other, and that our continuing development in life is the product of maintaining a healthy tension between the two.

Modes of Commitment

Since the fifth century B.C.E., when Hippocrates classified human beings on the basis of their "bodily humors," (choleric, melancholic, phlegmatic, and sanguine) there have been scores of efforts to categorize the variety of human personalities. In understanding the commitments that stem from our strivings for actuation and participation, however, none seems more relevant than the typology of Eduard Spranger, a member of the "culture science" school of psychology which arose in Germany following World War I.

Spranger set out to describe various types of human beings by isolating and idealizing each of the "value-tendencies" he saw at work in people. His conclusions became the basis for the *Study of Values* developed by Allport, Vernon, and Lindsey at Harvard University.

Spranger hypothesized that individuals fall into one or more of six types of personalities. While he does not describe these in terms of agency and communion, it seems to me that three of them lead to commitments of actuation, three to commitments of participation. While all of us embody all six of the values he describes, our personalities tend to focus on one or two areas more than on the others.

The six types of personalities he discovered are:

1. Political
2. Economic
3. Theoretic
4. Social
5. Aesthetic, and
6. Religious

The Political personality is engaged in the search for *power* because power provides freedom, especially freedom of will.

The Economic personality is focused on *utility*, i.e. the usefulness of forces or products in satisfying needs, because utility affords freedom of action.

The Theoretic personality seeks *knowledge* about the laws and principles governing the universe, so that he or she can be "armed with understanding."

The Social personality enriches himself or herself through the enrichment of others. For this person the highest value is *love* because it provides personal fulfillment.

The Aesthetic personality is motivated by the will to create form or *beauty*. *Impressions* gained through the five senses are translated into *expressions*, which furnish a different kind of fulfillment.

The Religious person seeks *meaning* above the other values. The capstone of this value is one's experience of the significance of individual existence.

Needless to say, the strongest value-tendency in any one of us tends to guide our perception. Observing a tree, the Aesthetic Person sees the form and beauty of its branches. The Economic Person sees lumber, or board feet.

In the same way, an assembly of people may be seen by the Political Person as a challenge to win them over, whereas the same people may be seen by the Social Person as the chance to build community.

A principle at work in nature or society may be seen by the Theoretic Person as a means of knowledge and authority, whereas the Religious Person may perceive order and meaning.

For Spranger, these six "life-forms" comprise the fundamental value-tendencies in human beings. I believe each of them leads toward a commitment of actuation or participation, depending on the realm of expression in which each is dominant. If that realm of expression is the *social* world, the striving for actuation results in the Political person, whereas the striving for participation produces the Social person.

If the realm is the *natural* world, the striving for actuation leads to the Economic person whereas the striving for participation leads to the Aesthetic person.

The third realm of expression is the *symbolic* world, the realm by which we interpret things to ourselves and others. Here the striving for actuation produces the Theoretic person, the striving for participation the Religious person.

The innate strivings that govern these six value-tendencies can be charted in a "values-matrix" as follows:

Form of Intentionality	Realm of Expression		
	Social World	Natural World	Symbolic World
Actuation	Political Mode	Economic Mode	Theoretic Mode
Participation	Social Mode	Aesthetic Mode	Religious Mode

TRUST IS THE ULTIMATE COMMITMENT

If commitment is the path to meaning, there is an especially powerful kind of commitment known as covenant. The word covenant may call to mind marriage, but a covenant can be any kind of binding agreement between parties. It can be a covenant as negative as one between neighbors to keep certain "undesirables" out of the community or as lofty as one between God and human beings.

Actually, in the early days of Judeo-Christian history, there were two kinds of covenants. One was the voluntary "covenant of parity" between two equals, in which either party could say yes or no.

More common in those days, however, was the "covenant of suzerainty" or sovereignty, in which a conqueror or ruler would make or force an agreement with a tribe or a people. The agreement was that the conqueror would protect the people from threats such as outside invaders and, in return, the people would pay tribute of some sort to their "lord," usually a portion of their crops or other resources.

This was not a covenant between equals. For the people, it was an "offer they couldn't refuse."

In the Hebrew Bible, this is the kind of covenant Moses saw God making with the Hebrew people. The way it was put was as follows:

"I am the Lord your God who brought you out of the land of Egypt, out of the house of bondage…(therefore) you shall have no other Gods before me."

That first commandment was followed by nine more, which we call the Ten Commandments.

The basis for the covenant was God's rescue of his people. The expectation was that the people in return would keep God's commands as to how they should live as a nation.

The results of that covenant were so mixed they required reminders on a regular basis that the people were not living up to God's expectations. Those reminders over the centuries came by way of the prophets (who were not fore-tellers so much as forth-tellers), most of whom were ignored or persecuted, telling the people not only how they were failing but how God was set on keeping his covenant.

Finally, in the seventh century B.C.E., one of those prophets, named Jeremiah, announced that the days were coming when a new covenant, not like the one on "tablets of stone" that the people had broken, would be "written on the hearts" of the whole people.

Centuries later, for those who believe that God was acting in Jesus of Nazareth, known to Christians as the "Messiah" (Hebrew for "the anointed one") or the "Christ" (the Greek translation of Messiah) this new covenant was sealed in the life, teaching, crucifixion, and resurrection of this same Jesus, who called himself "the Son of Man" (we would say the Human One). Indeed, he told his followers as he poured wine at their last supper together that "this is my blood of the covenant, which is poured out for many."

Moreover since God, in Paul Tillich's words, is the "ground of our being" or, as described in the Biblical book of Acts, "the one in whom we live and move and have our being," it follows that a commitment to the God whom Christians believe revealed his nature and purpose in Jesus is the ultimate commitment we can make, the one which gives meaning to all the other commitments we make.

Ultimate trust in this God stems from and results in the knowledge that we live in a meaningful, purposeful universe governed by the One who loves each one of us with a fierce intensity. That love, however, is experienced only in our making this commitment of trust! For the person who enjoys this trust, the rest can seem like idle conversation.

Peter Berger suggests that the religious impulse, "the quest for meaning that transcends the restricted space of empirical existence in this world, has been a perennial feature of humanity." Augustine said it more directly: "Our hearts are restless until they find their rest in God."

Faith and Trust: The Distinction

The concept of faith is too often understood as adherence to a set of beliefs about God. Trust, on the other hand, is not a belief system or even in one sense a religion, but rather a relationship. It is nothing more – and nothing less – than confidence in the person and work of the living God.

Albert Einstein said there is one basic question in life: Is the universe friendly? I believe the answer is that it is. And since friendship is a personal relationship, it follows (1) that the universe is essentially *personal* and (2) that our God is a personal God.

The other problem with the concept of faith is that it is too often seen as a dependent, one-way relationship between man and God, which is only half the truth. The fact is that while human beings do depend on God, it is also true that the competent and caring God whom Jesus of Nazareth called Father depends on humans to keep the covenant He has made with us.

At its worst, religion confines and restricts trust to belief. While religion can and does "bind" people together (which is the meaning of religion) trust is necessarily individual -- it means to trust with all of one's heart, mind, soul, and strength. It is the "meta-commitment" which holds together all our other commitments.

All of Christian theology, therefore, deals simply with the nature and implications of the mutual trust between humans and God.

Another problem in thinking about Christianity as a belief system rather than a relationship is that it gives us the impression that the more we know about someone the more control we have of that relationship but, as anyone in a serious relationship can tell you, relationships cannot *be* controlled, only appreciated and enjoyed (or unappreciated and rejected).

In a word, then, as human beings we make commitments in just three areas, (1) those of actuation or agency, (2) those of participation or communion, and (3) those of ultimate concern. These are the commitments to **work, love,** and **trust**.

Since all three of these commitments seem to end in death, it can be said they are imperiled by the existential threat of death, which they are. But we tend to think of only one kind of death -- physical death. In the language of trust, however, there is another kind of death, and that is our dying to the two main centers of our security and identity, namely the narrow, preoccupied *self* and the strictly material values of the *world,* i.e. the dominant values of the culture to which we belong.

But without this death to the self as ego and the world's values there is no way we can be prepared for a new *kind* of life of trust in the Spirit.

I use the term Spirit because Spirit is the source and destiny of all humans who are, above all else, spirits (with a small "s)." You will remember, in fact, that the Biblical position is (1) that "God is Spirit," and (2) that humans are "made in the image of God." These are, of course, statements of trust that the stuff of matter, which we encounter every day, is simply "spirit dancing" and that death, therefore, is not necessarily the end of human consciousness.

Until we encounter the existential fact of death, however, we don't take this first death -- dying to the narrow self or ego-- very seriously. Only then, if we are desperate for answers, do we turn to the One we call God.

I believe it can be said, in fact, that the existential reality of physical death is a huge wake-up call and, in fact, a favor to any reflective human being.

Marcus Borg reminds us that "the only reality about which our cultural world is certain is the visible world of our ordinary experience." Accordingly, it looks to the material world for satisfaction and meaning. But the dominant values of that world are what Borg calls the three A's: Achievement, Affluence, and Appearance.

You and I are certainly *in* that world. But we cannot hope to find ultimate meaning or purpose if we are entirely *of* that world.

That meaning and purpose can be found only in a living relationship with the One who *is* life, now and always.

How do we know this One, this Spirit who is truly life?

There are not one but many paths to "the One." In our own cultural, historical and geographical domain, we can come to know God through nature and an awesome universe. (Think of Elizabeth Barrett Browning's observation that "Earth's crammed with heaven, and every common bush afire with God; but only he who sees takes off his shoes. The rest sit round it and pluck blackberries.")

But because we understand God to be not just the author of the universe but also *personal* in nature (again, a statement of trust) we cannot help but wonder what God is like. And I believe the answer lies, as suggested before, in the history and experience of a particular people, the Hebrews.

That experience began with a man named Abraham in southern Mesopotamia almost 4,000 years ago, who felt called by God to go out, not knowing where he was going, to a "promised land" called Canaan. (Because of his trust, Abraham became the father of three great religions: Judaism, Christianity, and Islam.) The experience continued some 500 years later, as described earlier, when Moses understood that *he* was called by the same God "Yahweh" (meaning "I Am") to free his people from slavery in Egypt and proceed to that "promised land."

Moses did not live to see the occupation of Canaan. But his successor Joshua did, in a bold, sweeping leap across the Jordan River which resulted in a military conquest and the settling of the land.

The period which followed in Hebrew history brought a succession of charismatic leaders called "judges" who appeared from time to time to help the people hold the land against invading predators. The people insisted, however, that the last judge, named Samuel, create a *religious kingdom* led by a prince named Saul. So the religious community became a political nation.

Under King David, who followed Saul about 1,000 B.C.E., the nation of Israel (named for Jacob or Israel, Abraham's grandson) became an empire, but not before a new kind of figure appeared in Israel known as *the prophets*. These "spokespersons for God" spoke truth to power for hundreds of years. In the 8th century, Amos, a shepherd from Tekoa, promised the priest of the king Jeroboam that God loved Israel and would therefore punish the people for their apostate religious practices which had replaced justice and righteousness.

Isaiah, a "troubler of Israel" to Ahaz under the latter's kingship in the 8th century B.C.E., continued to speak against the national religion. "In quietness and trust shall be your strength," he said.

And so the pattern of trust vs. religion continued throughout the history of Israel. In the sixth century B.C.E., the prophet known as second Isaiah, speaking during the conquest and exile of the Hebrew people to Babylon, followed by their return after 50 years, saw Israel as God's suffering servant, called to be a "light to the nations" of the earth.

The Biblical books of wisdom, too, such as Job, focused on trust in God and not in religious works, or even religious attitudes. And the Psalms, those moving hymns of the second temple, are filled with calls to trust.

But none of these were as compelling for both Jews and Gentiles who followed the "Way" of Jesus of Nazareth, who saw in his life, death, and resurrection some two thousand years ago the model for trust in God. Indeed, there is something so winsome, so compelling, and so *present* about this Jewish carpenter and itinerant teacher that for many he *had* to be the living embodiment and revelation of God.

In this same Jesus, those of us who believe in a loving, faithful God see the nature of God himself. And while we see Jesus as "God's Word" (*logos*) and "Truth incarnate," we believe that he was also fully human. The fact is that Jesus called himself the "Son of Man" which, in contemporary language, means the "Human Being" or "Human One.".

What's more remarkable about this authentic human being, however, is that while he may have been the first of a new humanity, his unabashed invitation was for those who follow him to join him in the *Family of the New Humanity*. In fact, he spoke of the "Son of Man" not just as an individual but as a corporate community, in which we are invited to be members. Trust is the one and only price of entry. And while membership in what Jesus called the "kingdom of God" (we would say the family of God) is freely given, it is not devoid of cost in being carried out, since its values are so different from those of the world.

The history of Christianity has been a continuation of the struggle between trust and its regular replacement by rigid belief systems, requiring, as in early Israel, returns and reformations to recover the relationship of God and human beings as one of trust, in fact of mutual trust. I say mutual trust because that is the kind of trust that Jesus practiced in his relationship to God as father or "Abba" (the Aramaic meaning is "Dad") in a covenant of parity rather than one of sovereignty.

The Psychological "Battle Within"

Gordon Allport, the Harvard psychologist who was one of the authors of the Study of Values referred to earlier, suggested there is a difference between what he called *intrinsic* religion and *extrinsic* religion (or what we would call *trust* and *observance*). For Allport, intrinsic religion characterizes persons who have *interiorized* their faith or trust. These people are intent on serving their religion rather than having it serve them although, being human, most of us probably share a mix of the two.

Extrinsic religion, on the other hand, tends to be a self-serving, utilitarian, self-protective kind of attitude which provides the follower with the comfort of "salvation." For the extrinsic believer, truth is rigid and absolute, being revealed once for all and not meant for tampering.

The problem in *defining* a commitment of personal trust in a living, loving God is that, in the final analysis, it cannot really be seen except through experience. Jesus, in describing the "kingdom of God," used parables or inferred analogies to describe this phenomenon. His message, however, was the "good news" or gospel of God's active presence and work in the world.

How does this come about for the individual? Perhaps the most succinct description of the process is to be found in the hymn written by a converted English slave-ship captain named John Newton entitled "Amazing Grace."

It was "grace that taught my heart to fear," he wrote, "and grace my fear relieved. How precious did that grace appear, the hour I first believed."

In other words, it seems it is only in an hour of desperation or peril that we turn in trust to the One who is present but unseen. And out of that first *experience* of trust we come to know God's presence and faithfulness and thereby to trust that love and presence not once but continually in life.

So we can share that good news with one another. But there is no way I know of in which we can share that experience. It is futile, in a way, to write or talk about trust as the ultimate commitment. There is no commitment more personal or more important in life, and surely no commitment which gives life more meaning.

Furthermore, there are many obstacles to the quest for this meaning-giving trust. Not the least of these is the "Babylonian captivity" of Christianity by self-appointed guardians who have turned an open-ended, experiential journey of the questing, questioning mind for the ultimate, un-nameable God into a fundamentalist, closed-minded, literalistic interpretation which understands neither metaphor nor analogy. It is something between sad and tragic that, for thoughtful seekers who value critical thinking, not to mention the capacities of their own minds, this hijacking of the faith can be a genuine stumbling block to inquiry.

For the seeker after meaning who can make a commitment of trust, on the other hand, the door may open to an experience of refreshment and reassurance that the God of amazing grace is the true and trustworthy lord of life -- and death.

Having begun, therefore, with the subject of death, let us conclude with the same subject. We will all die sooner or later, some of us sooner than later. Like Abraham, we will be called to "go out, not knowing where we are going." Will we die in fear or in trust? The answer may depend on whether we have found that trust is possible, and reliable, and have learned to *live* in trust. When the time comes, it will surely be helpful to have had some practice in the process.

COMMITMENTS THAT GENERATE MEANING

The First Commitment: To Love

I have just lost a lovely and loving wife, to whom I was married for seventy years. It was, for me, a beautiful marriage of two independent yet interdependent people. So I now feel as if I'm living only half a life. But that only strengthens my conviction there is nothing so rewarding as a life lived in love.

On the other hand, it needs to be said that love is either the most dynamic or the most useless word in the English language. It is certainly the most overused, the most abused, and probably the least understood word in the English language, thanks in large part to its ambiguity. But then to expect a single word to carry so many different meanings was probably futile from the start. It might help, then, if we spoke Greek.

The Greek language had many different words for the various meanings of "love," which would be useful these days. *Storge* was used to communicate family or kinship connection, an affection generated through familiarity (which has the same root as family). *Philia* described social or brotherly love, i.e. the bond between friends. *Eros* denoted sexual or romantic love, or any love elicited by the desirability of its object. *Agape*, which was free of association with the first three meanings just mentioned, meant *caring* (caritas in Latin), the unconditional kind of love that seeks to help the one or ones who are loved.

In a word, then (or four words), *storge* meant self-connecting love, *eros* self-seeking love, *philia* self-sharing love, and *agape* self-giving love.

The one thing they had in common, however, was that love is the passion that animates the world.

In a letter to the Christian community at Corinth, the apostle Paul wrote that "Love (*agape*) is patient and kind; love is not jealous or boastful; it is not irritable or resentful; it does not rejoice in the wrong but rejoices in the right. Love bears all things, believes all things, hopes all things, endures all things."

Is there any description of love more inclusive or more conclusive than this?

The reason love is the first and foremost commitment in life is that loving and being loved is the most dependable source of joy in living. Jesus taught that if you want to find life, you must give your life away, whereas if you cling to life you will lose it. And what else is love if it isn't giving your life away.

What are the characteristics of love? First of all, genuine love is not transitory but *permanent*. It doesn't burn hot or cold but is like a steady flame that lights the heart. The covenants, whether between God and humankind, or between human beings, are not destined for death but are endless. "The grass withers, the flowers fade," but authentic love is endless.

Secondly, love is not general but *particular*. There is a line that goes "How odd of God to choose the Jews." But it's not odd at all. We choose the ones we love, and God decided not only that these would be his people but that it was through this particular people he would reach out to all people. The particularity of love holds as true today as ever. We think we can love everyone but that does little for anyone unless we love someone, or a set of someones, in particular.

I remember in the 1960's a student organization called the Student Nonviolent Coordinating Committee, or SNCC. I met some of its members and there was no doubt they loved humanity. But I learned that some of them, at least, had a really difficult time relating to individuals. Love is not like that. If you can't love an individual in particular, how are you going to love humanity in general.

Third, love is *palpable*. It leaves a mark on any of us it finds. Like any other commitment, it tends to be contagious, as is the absence of love. I believe it is safe to say that if we have never had the experience of being loved, it will be difficult for us to love anyone but ourselves. But if someone at some point has given us something approaching unconditional love, it is also safe to say it is likely we will exercise that same kind of love at some point in our lives, perhaps throughout our lives.

Much has been written about love over the centuries. In the book *Forty Thousand Quotations*, most topics are covered in a few lines or on a page or two. On the topic of love, however, there are ten pages of quotations, from "Love must be as much a light as a flame." (Thoreau) to "It is better to have loved and lost than never to have loved at all."(Tennyson) But the most soaring tributes to love are found in the Bible, such as the one above from Paul's letter to the Corinthians.

It is hard to speak of love without mentioning sex, since sex can be (though not necessarily so) an expression of love.

Sex in the public sphere these days seems to be more of a commodity, however, than an expression of love. In a time when we are urged to let candor reign, we seem to be letting sex reign over love instead of love reigning over sex. To Sigmund Freud we owe the distorted picture of sex as relief or release from sexual tension rather than as a factor in the attraction – and attachment – of one unique person to another. So much for romance, which is, at least in this culture, the stimulus to monogamy and frequently a lifetime of companionship and fidelity.

The question is whether we seek sex with an object or sex with another human being. If it's the former, it really has little to do with love. Almost any object will do. If it's the latter, then the potential for love is great.

As Viktor Frankl has written, "The potential of human sex consists in its becoming an embodiment of love." When that is true, it is because love seeks completion or wholeness. Again, with Frankl, "I do not use another human being but I encounter him, which means I recognize his humanness" and going a step further, "if I recognize his uniqueness as a person… what then takes place is love."

Here once again we are faced with the question of whether to look for explanations to our instincts and drives (which are causes coming from the past) or to meanings (which are linked to reasons and the future).

Does this mean that love depends on sex? Not at all. One can love another or many others without expectation of return. But that grows out of empathy rather than an expectation of symmetry.

What more can be said about love? Only that without it, the world would be a dismal place indeed, whereas with it life can generate meaning beyond human understanding.

The Second Commitment: To Work

If love fulfills the striving for communion, or participation, it is work that fulfills the striving for agency, or actuation. It can even be said that our work, whether for better or worse, is our signature on the world.

The question is what is meaningful work, i.e. work which creates meaning in our lives and the lives of others? E.F. Schumacher seeks to answer that question in his book, *Good Work*.

Good work, he writes, is (1) that which produces necessary goods and services for society; (2) that which enables us to use and perfect our skills and gifts; (3) that which liberates us from our built-in egocentricity.

In the same way that our handwriting, according to graphologists, reveals our personality to those who know how to read it, so the work we choose, or are chosen by, reveals who we are and what we want our legacy to be.

Is there such a thing as a *calling* to do a certain kind of work? And if so, what is so compelling about that calling?

The idea of calling has been around since time began. But it was central to the thinking of Martin Luther, a leader of the Protestant Reformation. Luther believed that every legitimate form of work, from that of the manager to the milkmaid, is of equal importance to God.

That perspective seems to confirm what Aristotle observed about happiness, that where our individual talents meets the world's needs, there we will find our calling. The reason is that happiness is paramount and that happiness comes in large part from the passion of living out what we are meant to do.

A concept important to an understanding of calling is that of spirit or *pneuma*, sometimes thought of as the realm of God-consciousness, which is parallel to the concept of *psyche*, the realm of self-consciousness where we find the mind and emotions.

The problem is that in this materialistic age we lack the vocabulary to speak about calling. Calling is about the human spirit and if we talk about spirit in our day it seems as if we are speaking an ancient and foreign language.

But talk we must because a sense of calling is not only the mark of a fulfilled and fulfilling life; it is also a function of the human spirit.

We know we have found our calling when we lose ourselves in our work.

We know we have found our calling when we can't wait for the day to begin.

We know we have found our calling when we are living to serve others.

We know we have found our calling when we are giving our lives away.

Our calling may, or may not, be the way we earn our living. But it will certainly be the way we find our life. And that's a mystery of the spirit. For if spirited work is life, dispirited work is death.

But what has happened to spirit in our time?

When Jesus of Nazareth (in the gospel of John) asked the Jewish leader Nicodemus whether he had been "born from above," he was asking whether Nicodemus, having been born once as a physical human being, had become aware that he was a spiritual being as well.

The question is important because making a commitment to work which embraces our whole being or spirit needs to arise from the purpose for which we live. And the goal of that discovery, which comes more often than not after the fact, is to know where our innate talents most closely meet the world's needs.

As for work that embraces the spirit, it is clear we have moved away from the transcendent toward the tangible and immediate. This shift may have had some merit in focusing on the material needs and pains of the world. But in making it, we have also moved away from our fundamental nature as spiritual beings. And in doing so we have largely lost or banned from our vocabulary the words to describe our existence as human spirits.

That may be because we can't really separate an understanding of human spirit from our understanding of God as Spirit.

The Hebraic expression of relationship to and kinship with God sought to preclude that separation. The mystery of the self, which includes not only body and mind but their summation in spirit, was described in the word for "breath" or "wind" (*ruach* in Hebrew, later as *pneuma* in Greek). To have breath or life was not to have spirit but to *be* spirit.

Since spirits act, or behave, however, we needed to know what to do, and what not to do. This was summed up in the Hebrew *shema*, "Hear, O Israel, the Lord God is One, and you shall love the Lord your God with all your heart, and mind, and strength." (The itinerant Jewish rabbi Jesus later linked that commandment with the one in Leviticus to "love your neighbor as yourself.") Based on the fact that God had freed the Israelites from bondage in Egypt, then, Israel was given the ten commandments and their ramifications known as "the Law." Even with frequent reminders by the prophets, however, Israel apparently failed to keep the Law which, in some ways, seemed to be a poverty-stricken master. Why? Because by itself it lacks internal power.

Spirit on the other hand has power because it connects not just with doing but with *being*. It has the force of *passion*. It does not do away with the Law. But it surpasses law in its ability to motivate behavior or action.

That is why Jesus focused not on rightness of action but on *rightness of being*, and loving, through Spirit. If you want to worship God who is Spirit, he said, you must do so in spirit and in truth.

If Frankl is right about the fact that what we need above all else is meaning, then the absence of meaning is not a disease of the mind or body but of the spirit. But if the spirit is unmentionable or inaccessible, i.e. if we don't see and cannot articulate the fact that we are spirit, it becomes impossible to extract meaning from it.

So how is human spirit related to Holy Spirit, another name for God, the Nameless One. How do the two interact if not in or through our existence in the world?

Herein lies the necessity to distinguish between human spirit and Holy Spirit. As for how we do that, theologian Arnold Come has written, "God has life in Himself, because he is eternally realized Spirit. Man must receive life as a gift because he only becomes spirit in dependence upon God."

The Unavoidable Commitment: To Find a Path Through Suffering

It may sound strange to connect suffering with commitment. But since it is hard to find anyone who has not suffered at one point or another in their lives, what do we do with the phenomenon of suffering, voluntary or involuntary, unless we can find meaning not in suffering itself but in our response to suffering.

It was suffering, in fact, under impossible conditions, which served as the matrix for Frankl's conclusion that suffering can be not only redemptive but also meaningful, and it was on this basis that he developed the concepts and practice of *logotherapy* (meaning therapy). During his experience in four different Nazi death-camps, Frankl found that while the outwardly strong prisoners often did not survive the deprivations and punishments of the camps, the weaker but inwardly strong and resourceful prisoners were able to survive because they had *the will to meaning*. In a far cry from Nietzsche's understanding of the phrase, Frankl concluded that "he who has a why to live can endure almost any how." He himself found meaning in recalling his wife's love, while enduring the torments of the camps, with the hope of reuniting with her someday.

To understand the heartache and the significance of suffering, it helps to be theologically attuned, especially to the Biblical prophet Isaiah, who lived and wrote during the almost 50-year exile of Israel to Babylon.

In chapters 40 to 55 of Isaiah (written by the one scholars call "Second Isaiah) there are four "Suffering Servant" songs, which progress from the notions of that one who suffers as Israel, as a light to the nations, to the servant as an individual, to the servant who is to come (the "Messiah" or anointed one) to the servant as a man of sorrows, to victory through suffering. Arguably the most beautiful poetry in the history of literature, there is no way to summarize these compelling songs in a short space. But an excerpt may be helpful:

> Behold my servant, whom I uphold,
>
> My chosen, in whom my soul delights;
>
> I have put my spirit upon him,
>
> He will bring forth justice to the nations.
>
> He will not cry or lift up his voice, or make it heard in the street;
>
> A bruised reed he will not break,

And a dimly burning wick he will not quench;

He will faithfully bring forth justice.

He will not fail or be discouraged

Until he has established justice in the earth.

(Isaiah 42: 1-4 Revised Standard Version)

It is not surprising, then, that those who embrace the Christian faith see Jesus of Nazareth, five hundred years later, as the realization of Isaiah's suffering servant. In fact, he opened his mission by quoting Isaiah and modeled this role in everything he said or did.

So can our response to suffering have a purpose? Can it have a promise?

Christianity believes it can. The Greek word *pathos* and its Latin derivative *passio* both have the meaning of endurance or suffering. Hence the suffering of Christ is understood as the passion of Christ.

Suffering, or consciousness of pain, has the value of teaching us patience and leading us to prayer. It tempers the spirit and instills a longing for "home" or permanence. It can also generate empathy, leading us to comfort others who suffer. The second beatitude (in Phillips' translation) is "Happy those who know what sorrow means. They shall be given courage and comfort." Or, in the RSV version, "Blessed are those who mourn; they shall be comforted."

In much the same way, the first of the Buddha's "four noble truths" is that *life IS suffering.* It is everywhere. It comes to everyone. Why is that so? How do we end it?

The second noble truth is that the cause of suffering (dukkha) is craving, thirst, or desire. But all of these are efforts to give us a sense of security in a world which is temporary and conditional.

The third noble truth, then, is that the end of suffering comes only with enlightenment or awakening.

The fourth noble truth is that we become enlightened by following the *wisdom* of a right view and right intention, the *ethical conduct* of right speech, action, and a right livelihood, and the *mental discipline* of right effort, mindfulness, and concentration, together constituting the eight-fold path to enlightenment.

If I were an atheist I would have a problem *from* suffering but not with the fact *of* suffering because suffering is simply a fact of life. But the Christian needs somehow to reconcile the reality of suffering with trust in a compassionate God, who may not will everything that happens but who certainly wills something *in* everything that happens.

We have all heard the argument that "if God is omnipotent and if God cares, why do humans suffer?"

The only answer to this dilemma lies, I believe, in two propositions:

1. In this world of imperfect human beings, suffering is inevitable.
2. In this world that belongs to a loving, suffering God, no one suffers alone.

Indeed, the God who sustains us in our suffering is the same God who confronts us with his own suffering on our behalf through his Christ on the cross.

If we can look at suffering from this broader perspective, i.e. if we trust that God suffers both with us and for us, we may find a meaningful response to that suffering, and the conviction that our suffering may have a purpose, even if we don't fully understand what that purpose may be for now.

In summary, while we find meaning in life from the commitments we make in (1) self-giving love and (2) life-enhancing "good work," the culmination of those commitments may be to give our lives away in the service of others, through suffering if necessary but surely with the steadfast hope for tomorrow during the years that we live and the legacy of hope for the future which will endure long after we are gone.

The apostle Paul in his letter to the Romans describes suffering as "tribulation, distress, persecution, famine, nakedness, peril, and the sword." But he claims that we are more than conquerors through him who loved us. "I am sure," he writes, "that neither death, nor life, nor angels, nor principalities, nor things present, nor things to come, nor powers, nor height, nor depth, nor anything else in all creation, will be able to separate us from the love of God in Christ Jesus our Lord." And if we are embraced by a loving, suffering God, we will never suffer alone.

For Paul, then, suffering has meaning because the trials we suffer are the way we come to trust in the God who cares for us beyond all measure.

THE CURIOUS DYNAMICS
OF COMMITMENT

Obstacles and Aids to Commitment

Commitments do not come easily. Nor should they. There are good and sound reasons for not making *any* commitment. One is that it keeps us from doing spontaneous, foolish things. The potential commitment to anything needs to be tested for both its profits and losses.

Perhaps the greatest obstacle to commitment is that it seems as if we are giving away a part of ourselves, which we are. And that doesn't seem very sensible on the face of it.

Jesus of Nazareth told his followers, however, that "whoever would save his life will lose it, and whoever loses his life for my sake (which is to say for the love of others) will find it."

My experience is that this is not so much a religious doctrine as a simple, existential truth. I have not met anyone who has practiced giving his or her life away for others who has not experienced a sense of fulfillment and meaning. Nor have I met anyone who has not practiced it who didn't seem to be leading something of a narrow, self-centered, and pinched existence.

Another obstacle to making a commitment is fear. Fear of the judgment of other people, or fear of one's own judgment.

I remember leaving the business world for theological seminary and then for parts unknown, and relinquishing what seemed like a guarantee of personal and financial stability for life, in order to pursue a new course of service instead of security. It was with great trepidation not only for myself but also for my family that I was jeopardizing their future, not just my own. This was compounded by the judgment of business colleagues who told me I was making the biggest mistake of my life. But there is nothing harder to resist than the "calling" that there is a different path that one must follow.

A third obstacle is that we really don't *know* something is the right thing until we have experienced it. It may be true that we need to live life looking forward, but it's also true that life can be understood only by looking back. Only in looking *back* can we be sure we have made the right decision about anything. That is where the question of *trust* comes in, which must be tested by what we have experienced in life up to that time.

Take wedding vows, for example. In a way they are not a commitment at all but rather a promise of future commitment that we make to the one we love, to ourselves, and to society, that we will not abandon that person for anyone else.

It is only *within* marriage, however, with its sorrows and joys, that we find the meaning of commitment. Only with endurance, flexibility, and continuity – along with the growth of both partners — does the commitment become real.

It is the same with our commitment to the living God. We cannot fully know the love and presence of God except from inside the wonder of the one whom Jesus called "Abba," the Aramaic equivalent not of a formal father but of one's personal "Dad."

It is only in that commitment that we come to know, in a poetic word, that:

For the things that really matter, you do not need a sign. You are loved so do not be afraid. I have called you by name, you are mine!

If there are obstacles to making commitments, however, there are aids as well. The chief aid is the quiet thoughtfulness which some call mindfulness, others prayer. There is a psalm that describes that state: "I bless God who is my counselor. And in the night my inmost self instructs me."

The greatest aid to a thoughtful commitment, therefore, is the surety which comes from open-minded reflection on the options that lie before us, followed by a listening patiently for that "still, small voice" which is likely to give us the answer.

The Two Realms of Commitment

If there are the two paths of actuation and participation which lead to commitment, there are also two realms in which to make them. One is the realm of the material world in which we live every day. The other is the spiritual world which is also with us constantly but which is accessible only when we open ourselves to the leading of the Spirit.

Both realms are important. But we must come to decide in which realm our ultimate meaning lies. Life in the spirit, sometimes called "the kingdom of

God," embraces quite different values from life in the material world.

If the values of the material world are wealth, power, and social approval, the values of the spiritual world are humility, simplicity, and empathy. Consider the beatitudes in the New Testament:

Happy are the humble-minded; the kingdom of God is theirs.

Happy those who know what sorrow means; they shall be given courage and comfort.

Happy those who claim nothing; the whole earth will be their possession.

Now how are the humble, the sorrowful, the meek supposed to be happy or blessed? Not just in the New Testament but in the minds and words of the Hebrew prophets, it was the poor, the dispossessed, the outcast, the widow, and the orphan who found favor in God's sight. They did not, as they already knew, have a favored place in the world. They were completely, desperately dependent on God. So it follows that they found special favor in God's realm, right here and now. Or is that an unimpeachable reason to be happy?

Commitments are Contagious

Because we are all both creatures of purpose and partners in the human enterprise, not to mention incurable mimics, it is not surprising that our commitments tend to be contagious, as is the passion that prompts them.

The founders of most movements in history have been people of passion and indomitable commitment. That is why they have disciples or followers, whether for better or worse or, in Richard Steele's words, whether they employ their passions in the service of life or their lives in the service of their passions.

One problem with the concept of passion is that in its current use it has so many meanings and conveys so many emotions, ranging from love to anger to desire. But in its original meaning in both Greek and Latin, passion meant suffering. Even today, in fact, Webster's first definition of passion is "the sufferings of Christ between the last supper and his death."

Are human beings good or evil? The unequivocal answer is "Yes." We are both. What is sometimes overlooked, however, is that the commitments we make, for good or for evil, are who we become.

Let me give you a personal example. I do not especially enjoy public speaking and I find exceptionally little joy in raising money. But when I decided to try to start a college I found I needed to put aside my avoidance of both those tasks.

I still didn't like public speaking or raising money. But these tasks, distasteful as they were, were soon swallowed up in my commitment. And the passion of that commitment often led to unexpected success.

I remember, for example, having luncheon one day with a member of the college's governing board which ended with his handing me a sizable check to complete a multi-million dollar fund-raising campaign for the campus we were building. So I asked him why he was doing this when he could have given this kind of support to any one of the other nonprofit organizations in which he played a role. His answer was that he had not met anyone as committed to any project as I was to this one. What that meant at the end of the day was that there were now two of us with the same dedication.

The same was true for many other good friends and companions on the way. It became clear very early that no individual can start a college. It takes a village of equally committed fellow travelers to create a college or anything else that is going to have lasting value. It still amazes me that the opportunity to develop something good for the world (as opposed to something good for an individual) can attract so many others who feel the same way. Commitments *are* contagious.

It is also true that all meaning-producing commitments are personal and relational, and that when it comes to fund-raising, the *Wall Street Journal* editorial was right: People do not give to causes; they give to *people*!

Looking back on life, it does not take a great deal of reflection to see that our commitments, for better or worse, have made us who we are, and that the commitments we are making here and now will determine who we will further become.

The small boarding school I attended as a youngster had a motto, in Latin of course. It was *Rebus Factis Agnoscamur.* As I remember that meant "By our deeds let us be known."

Since we are all meaning-making beings, and since we are governed more by our intentions than by our actions, perhaps that motto should be revised to read, "By our commitments let us be known."

The Timing of Commitments

When the 1960's hit "Turn! Turn! Turn!" was written by Pete Seeger in the late 1950's, it was the first time a large portion of the Scriptures (these written in the 3rd century BCE) had been turned into a popular folk song. That may have been partially due to the fact that those living in the 1960's believed their period was an especially significant time.

"To everything there is a season, and a time to every purpose under heaven." Thus went the lyrics.

This philosophy about time, in turn, was a reflection of the Hebrew tradition that time is not strictly sequential or ordinary, which is the way we see it when we think of chronological time. There are also extraordinary or special times for special occasions or, for that matter, special commitments.

Once again, the Greeks had a word (or two words) for it. The word for chronological time was *chronos*. The word for appropriate or opportune time was *kairos*.

Jesus meant this kind of time when he said "My time has not yet come." He also meant it when he inaugurated his mission with the words, "The time is fulfilled, and the kingdom of God is at hand."

That is true for us, as well. There are kairotic times in our lives when we are called to make decisions about commitments, and once past they may be gone forever. So it's important to be aware, and to be prepared, when we sense we are called to commit ourselves to some particular decision or action.

When the heart and mind and spirit are aligned, that is the moment. That's especially true for the heart, which is the core of the Hebrew understanding of the force which motivates us to do something. In Pascal's words, "The heart has reasons that reason cannot know."

Along with the heart goes the spirit, if our spirit is one of discernment. It is well to obey the mind, as well, but the mind usually confirms what the heart and spirit already know.

LIFE AS A CHAIN OF COMMITMENTS

If meaning is our goal in life, we won't find it by pursuing meaning. That will be counterproductive.

The pursuit of meaning is like the pursuit of happiness (enshrined along with the pursuit of life and liberty in the U.S. Declaration of Independence). It can't be found by looking for it.

If we want to find meaning, we need to consider the commitments we have made, are making, or plan to make. Commitments are the only path to meaning. If they are life-affirming and feed our spirit, we are on the right path. Without a significant commitment, we face what Viktor Frankl calls an "existential vacuum."

That sounds simple but the fact is that meaning, like love, is *particular* to the individual. No two persons will find precisely the same meaning for their lives. Frankl, for example, was once told what he had already discovered, that the meaning in his life came from helping others to find the meaning in theirs.

Something Jewish rabbis have known for a long time is that *the truth is in the story* i.e. our story, the story we choose, or are chosen by, to live. I believe we can best understand the arc of that story only by looking at the commitments we have made or are making. If, as Socrates said, the unexamined life is not worth living, perhaps an examined life can help us understand.

It is said that the apple doesn't fall very far from the tree. That is probably true of my family. My father was an achiever. Born in a small Virginia town, he was the second child in a brood of nineteen, and the only one of the nineteen who accepted the chance to go to college and, after that, law school in Washington, D.C., where he had a successful practice for decades and was Secretary of the Bar Association.

My mother was an achiever, too. An only child, she yearned to be a concert singer and, soon after I was born, she attended the American Conservatory in Fontainebleau, France, to study with the world-famous Walter Damrosch.

Whether it was their example or something in our DNA, my own striving to achieve seemed important, probably as a way of finding acceptance. By acceptance, I mean finding positive answers to such questions as "Am I worthy to be liked, or loved? More fundamentally, "Is my existence justified?"

Needless to say, there are two kinds of acceptance: conditional and unconditional. Psychologist Carl Rogers defined conditional acceptance as that which is based not on who we are but what we do. In the first thirty years of my life, it was this kind of acceptance I understood and strived to win.

My parents were divorced when I was seven, but that wasn't a great a shock to me since my mother's mother Jean was a loving, caring grandmother. With her and my mother I grew up in Connecticut, where I attended a small boarding school for boys. I was the school's bugler, edited its paper, and was a diligent student.

While I did not encounter death in the family when I was a boy, I apparently thought about it, because I recently came across a poem I wrote on an early birthday:

Vanished at last. Youth is done.

Faded the past, its victories won.

Destiny waits one last event.

Death is fearful. The fates are bold.

Age comes and life is spent.

My God, I am all of nine years old.

One of my boyhood commitments was to memorize and recite in a school assembly all eighteen pages of Coleridge's "Rhyme of the Ancient Mariner."

Another was the commitment to read, when I was 12, all 51 volumes of the Harvard Classics, although I was too young to understand many of them.

Since my school encouraged students to move at their own pace, I finished high school at 14 and applied to Harvard College, where I was accepted. But I decided I was too young for such a sophisticated place and opted instead to go to Bucknell University, a small, less worldly college in the heart of Pennsylvania.

In college, with a double major in English and History, I edited the school paper, sang in the men's glee club, played trumpet in the college band, worked in the dean's office, and waited table in my fraternity house. A Phil Beta Kappa graduate at 18, I moved to Philadelphia to work with N.W. Ayer & Son, Inc., a leading national advertising agency.

(All of these choices were, I believe, products of the striving for agency or *actuation*, motivated largely by a sense of the need for acceptance.)

A year after starting my first job, expecting to be drafted by the Army (it was during World War II), I volunteered instead for the Navy and completed officer's training at Columbia University as a newly minted ensign. Assigned to a submarine-chaser based at Treasure Island in San Francisco, I met and married, in the space of four months, a beautiful teacher at San Mateo High School who was working for the summer at Treasure Island. (This must have been motivated, as least in part, by the striving for communion or *participation.)*

Most of the rest of the war I spent on a U.S. Navy destroyer, assigned to convoy duty in the North Atlantic Ocean and then to the invasions of Normandy on D-Day and of Southern France.

When the war ended, I returned to Ayer as a Copywriter on advertising for A.T.& T. and other major accounts. I was then made an Associate Copy Director overseeing other writers, and was finally appointed to the newly created post of Creative Director in Detroit, Michigan, supervising a team of writers, art directors, and other creative staff. (More activities in the quest for actuation.)

During these years, I found the meaning in my life came from two sources. One was the family of a loving wife and two thoughtful daughters, from whose growth and development I derived great participatory joy. The other, alternatively, was the significant satisfaction I found in my own development as a writer and manager of creative people. The alternation and complementarity of these two strivings made life good and full.

The Journey from Achieving to Believing

Achieving in order to be accepted and achieving *because* we are accepted are motivations of an entirely different order. (The only challenge lies, in Paul Tillich's words, in learning to accept our own unconditional acceptance). In any case, it was only when I reached my thirties that the former changed to the latter and the question of ultimate meaning arose.

The occasion was my father's death of a heart attack on a train returning to Washington, D.C. from a vacation in Florida. I flew to Florida to help make arrangements for his return, the culmination of which were his memorial service in Washington and burial at Arlington National Cemetery.

It wasn't his death, however, that made me think about leaving the business world. It was rather that in his death I encountered the stark fact that I, too, would die, and felt that I could not leave this life without a sense that my life had greater meaning.

Even though I had never thought of myself as a "religious" person, I started asking myself such meaning questions as *Who am I? What shall I do with the rest of my life? What happens to us when we die?*

For some reason, I decided the best place to explore these questions might be a theological seminary, though I wasn't sure what a seminary was, had never visited one, and had no interest in preparing for a career in the ministry, which is the purpose of most such schools.

After a few years of mulling it over, however, I resigned from Ayer and enrolled in San Francisco Theological Seminary, a Presbyterian graduate school in northern California, making a commitment of three years for the intense study of Hebrew, Greek, Biblical Studies,

Theology, Psychology, Church History, and related fields.

My first reaction on leaving Ayer was that perhaps I had lost my mind, or at least my bearings. Ayer was an old and prestigious company which had brought ethics to the advertising business in 1869 and was a remarkably thoughtful firm for which to work. I derived much satisfaction from the work I was doing and my compensation had increased to the point where I could see a future guaranteed to provide our family of four with an enviable income and a lifestyle to which we could easily have become accustomed. To go out not knowing where I was going made no logical sense; it was just something I had to do.

(Having made the commitments of love and work, it seemed time to make a commitment of trust which required – and found – the support of the family in this seemingly irrational decision.)

Three years later I completed the M.Div. degree *summa cum laude* and having no interest in the parish ministry, which is what most graduates did, I thought perhaps I should return to the business world. I was asked by the placement counselor, however, whether I had ever considered working on a college campus. Again, I didn't know what that meant, but a few months later wound up at Portland State University, a commuter school of about 10,000 students, where I worked with five other campus ministers or university pastors from many different denominations to develop an ecumenical ministry and build a single new ecumenical campus center which offered jointly run programs for all students and faculty.

During my seven years in this role, I found in myself a great empathy for students in commuter universities who generally went from home to school to work with little time to develop friendships or, for that matter, to develop their own characters as distinctive, whole human beings.

So, seeking to sharpen my understanding of the field of higher education, I enrolled in the doctoral program in higher education at the University of California in Berkeley.

Several years later, when I'd completed the Ph.D. degree, I interviewed for positions at experimental colleges at several universities. But my concern was that those universities were focused chiefly on research and publishing rather than on individual student development, and it was likely that the experimental colleges so popular then, which ran counter to the university culture, would wind up on the trash heap which, after the radical sixties, most of them did.

The only answer seemed to be founding a college whose culture was devoted to individual student development. The result was an accredited work-study, world-study undergraduate school known as World College West. (The striving for agency or actuation really never goes away.)

The three kinds of experience built into the four-year liberal arts degree program were (1) the experience of participating in one's own education (all classes were small seminars); (2) the experience of study in a non-western culture for a year – the first semester in a home-stay and classes with our own faculty, the second semester on an approved independent project in a remote third-world village (a kind of academic "Peace Corps" experience in Mexico, China, Nepal, or Russia) and (3) an internship in the field of work in which the student was most interested.

To underscore the collegial nature of the school, we shunned conventional titles such as president and vice-president. My title was that of Spokesperson, the chief academic officer was known as the Coordinator of Studies, and the chief financial officer was the Coordinator of Resources. The problem was that the hierarchical model is so ingrained in the American psyche that few people understood what we were talking about. So much later we resorted to conventional titles.

After seven years we undertook the building of a new campus on 194 acres of pristine, rolling hills in Marin County, just north of San Francisco, which we had purchased when the college began. Construction of the campus included a mile-long road rising from sea-level to 400 feet. All utilities were installed underground, including a high-voltage electric system, conduit for up to 2,000 telephone, computer, and data lines, a mile-long 8-inch diameter water line to the top of the campus, a hidden 200,000-gallon water tank, and an innovative sewage-treatment system using transpiration by plants and evaporation by the sun to process 5,000 gallons of effluent a day.

The buildings of cedar and glass were nestled into the trees and hills, so no major trees were felled, and were heated and cooled with passive solar design for energy-savings of 75%.

The environmental design of the campus served not only as a beautiful setting for a collegial learning commmunity but also as a model for the B.A. degree itself in International Environmental Studies; International Service & Development; Art and

Society; Meaning, Culture, & Change; or International Business. The campus construction, built on a pay-as-you-go basis, was debt-free.

Over the years, there was substantial evidence that the college had achieved many of its goals. It was accredited by the Western Association of Schools and Colleges.

Barron's *Guide to the Best, Most Popular, and Most Exciting Colleges* named World College West, which it categorized as "very competitive," one of America's 368 "most notable schools." The college was commended for its special spirit and its focus on the international issues facing a world of limited natural resources.

Kiplinger's Changing Times ran a story entitled "The Best of the Bargain Colleges" in which the college was selected by thirteen experts as one of the 42 "highest quality, lowest cost colleges in the country."

The college being poised after fifteen years for its second stage of growth, and my having undergone open-heart surgery (and with parents both of whom died at the age of 62), I announced I would retire in a year at the age of 65. So the board undertook a year-long presidential search which attracted more than 100 applicants and the selection of one of them as president. From then on I had no role in the school's affairs, which is the norm in higher education. But my understanding, since confirmed, was that over the next four years several large loans were taken, with the debt-free campus as collateral, and that when no more could be borrowed the college was closed and the campus put up for sale.

What do you do when you have committed yourself and others toward what was to have been a promising end, only to find that what you thought would be permanent had vanished, except for the difference it may have made in the lives of the thousand or so people -- students, faculty members, staff members, board members, and donors who had given $13 million of their resources to help create a truly distinctive, collaborative learning community on a beautiful, ecological campus?

Since the educational philosophy that *learning through disciplined reflection on experience* had proved to be far more effective than either reflection or experience alone, however, the answer seemed to be that it should be done again!

So after a year of grieving, since we had committed all of our energy and assets to this venture during its first fifteen years, I incorporated another school based on the same educational philosophy. (Once again, a commitment of trust.)

The result was what is now independently accredited Presidio Graduate School, which has been in operation for more than 20 years. It pioneered the field of sustainable management and now, under competent and committed leadership, offers various certificates and "masters degrees with meaning," including the M.B.A. (Business Administration) and the M.P.A. (Public Administration) in Sustainable Management, in which every course teaches the integration of environmental, social, and financial concerns into the decisions we make in business, public, or nonprofit organizations.

The graduate programs started in 2003 with 22 students and a handful of faculty. There are now more than 40 faculty and staff and about 800 graduates who are leading the sustainability movement in firms around the world such as Alcatel-Lucent and Walmart. At this writing, in fact, Presidio Graduate School is ranked # 1 for sustainability and # 3 for social impact (in a tie with Yale University) according to a study by Net Impact of more than 3,000 students at 108 innovative graduate schools around the world.

There in a few pages you have a chronicle of the commitments which have given a lifetime of meaning to the author of this little volume.

If life is meant to be a chain of commitments which give meaning to that life, we have been blessed indeed.

Where does that chain of commitments lead which give zest and passion to our lives? In his seminal book, *The Force of Character*, James Hillman suggests that we become more characteristic of who we are simply by lasting into our later years. The older we become, the more our true natures emerge. "Character is to the late years," he writes, "as individual calling is to the early years; it gives sense and purpose to the changes of aging."

It is clear that the meaning in my life has come from the commitments (1) to love and be loved by a beautiful, caring wife for seventy years and the family we both cherished, and (2) to help create innovative, collaborative learning communities in which everyone learns from everyone else.

But it is also clear that the meaning which has held together these other meanings, has been trust in a loving, caring God who, in Jesus' words, will "never leave us orphans." The journey of turning, and constantly returning, to this source of our being has been a journey filled with promise that never ends.

You will remember that the title of this volume is *Passion before Prudence.*

What does that mean? It means that if we choose the path toward *meaning* before the path toward *security*, we will find fulfillment in life.

So do we discount prudence, or security, altogether? No, but if our choice lies between meaning and security, we will do well to choose the former over the latter.

In the words of Robert Frost:

"Two roads diverged in a wood, and I –

I took the one less traveled by,

And that has made all the difference."